POSITIVES

JOURNAL

A COMPANION WORKBOOK TO BRAIN TRAINING
FOR THE HIGHLY SENSITIVE PERSON

JULIE BJELLAND, LMFT

Designed by Jeanly Fresh M. Zamora

ISBN-13: 978-1-9762-4276-2

DEDICATION

This book is dedicated to all of you who are working to find yourself, love and accept yourself, and live an authentic life being "YOU."

CONTENTS

INTRODUCTION

This Positives Journal, a companion workbook to *Brain Training for the Highly Sensitive Person,* is designed to help you recognize and celebrate the positives in your life and learn to identify and implement activities that improve your mental, emotional, and physical well-being.

I hope this positives companion workbook can be something you turn to when you need to fill up your positive tank. Everything in this journal is positive and hopefully gives you a good feeling whenever you look at it. Think of it as a supportive friend that can be with you whenever you need a boost and reminder of all your positives.

Use this companion workbook each week as you learn and practice the brain-training techniques laid out in the book. This workbook is a place for you to record all of your successes, your strengths, and your gifts. You will use the Challenges and Growth Journal companion workbook to record your emotional triggers, your fears, and the areas of growth you are seeking. Acknowledging your challenges while focusing on and developing your positives will help you become the YOU you were meant to be.

WEEK ONE REFLECTIONS

Ask a few people with whom you are close to email you a list of what they see as positives about you. Record these lists in the space provided here.

_____

_____

_____

_____

_____

_____

_____

_____

_____

_____

_____

_____

_____

_____

_____

_____

_____

_____

_____

Write a message to yourself explaining why you are proud of yourself for choosing to make this positive, life-transforming change.

_____

_____

_____

_____

_____

_____

_____

Write the positive improvements you hope to achieve by implementing the brain-training techniques discussed in the book.

_____

_____

_____

_____

_____

_____

_____

Develop at least one personal goal that you want to achieve.

_____

_____

_____

_____

_____

_____

_____

_____

WEEK TWO REFLECTIONS

What are three things you are grateful for?
Do this for as many consecutive days as you can.

_____

_____

_____

_____

_____

_____

_____

_____

Now that you understand what is happening in your brain, can you find some compassion for yourself? How can you start being kinder and more loving toward yourself, even if it's just a little bit for now?

Remember, keep what you write in this journal positive.

_____

_____

_____

_____

_____

_____

_____

_____

Sunday

Today, I am grateful for . . .

_____

_____

_____

_____

_____

_____

_____

_____

I am proud of myself today because . . .

_____

_____

_____

_____

_____

_____

_____

_____

Monday

Today, I am grateful for . . .

_____

_____

_____

_____

_____

_____

_____

_____

I am proud of myself today because . . .

_____

_____

_____

_____

_____

_____

_____

_____

Tuesday

Today, I am grateful for . . .

_____

_____

_____

_____

_____

_____

_____

_____

I am proud of myself today because . . .

_____

_____

_____

_____

_____

_____

_____

_____

Wednesday

Today, I am grateful for . . .

_____

_____

_____

_____

_____

_____

_____

_____

_____

I am proud of myself today because . . .

_____

_____

_____

_____

_____

_____

_____

_____

_____

Thursday

Today, I am grateful for . . .

_____

_____

_____

_____

_____

_____

_____

_____

_____

I am proud of myself today because . . .

_____

_____

_____

_____

_____

_____

_____

_____

_____

Friday

Today, I am grateful for . . .

_____

_____

_____

_____

_____

_____

_____

_____

_____

I am proud of myself today because . . .

_____

_____

_____

_____

_____

_____

_____

_____

_____

Saturday

Today, I am grateful for . . .

_____

_____

_____

_____

_____

_____

_____

_____

_____

I am proud of myself today because . . .

_____

_____

_____

_____

_____

_____

_____

_____

_____

Additional Thoughts

WEEK THREE REFLECTIONS

What are three ways you can practice self-compassion?

_____

_____

_____

_____

_____

_____

_____

_____

List examples of ways that practicing self-compassion helps you fill up your positive tank more.

_____

_____

_____

_____

_____

_____

_____

_____

Write two encouraging and supportive things to yourself. (Think about how you would support a friend or loved one.)

_____

_____

_____

_____

_____

_____

_____

Practice validating your emotions here. For example, "I allow all of my emotions and care for myself in loving ways when I need more tenderness."

_____

_____

_____

_____

_____

_____

_____

Sunday

Today, I am grateful for . . .

_____

_____

_____

_____

_____

_____

_____

_____

I am proud of myself today because . . .

_____

_____

_____

_____

_____

_____

_____

_____

_____

Monday

Today, I am grateful for . . .

_____

_____

_____

_____

_____

_____

_____

_____

I am proud of myself today because . . .

_____

_____

_____

_____

_____

_____

_____

_____

Tuesday

Today, I am grateful for . . .

_____

_____

_____

_____

_____

_____

_____

_____

_____

I am proud of myself today because . . .

_____

_____

_____

_____

_____

_____

_____

_____

_____

Wednesday

Today, I am grateful for . . .

_____

_____

_____

_____

_____

_____

_____

_____

I am proud of myself today because . . .

_____

_____

_____

_____

_____

_____

_____

_____

Thursday

Today, I am grateful for . . .

_____

_____

_____

_____

_____

_____

_____

_____

I am proud of myself today because . . .

_____

_____

_____

_____

_____

_____

_____

_____

Friday

Today, I am grateful for . . .

_____

_____

_____

_____

_____

_____

_____

_____

I am proud of myself today because . . .

_____

_____

_____

_____

_____

_____

_____

_____

Saturday

Today, I am grateful for . . .

_____

_____

_____

_____

_____

_____

_____

_____

_____

I am proud of myself today because . . .

_____

_____

_____

_____

_____

_____

_____

_____

_____

Additional Thoughts

WEEK FOUR REFLECTIONS

What makes your stress numbers lower each day?
Try to be conscious of this every day.

_____

_____

_____

_____

_____

_____

_____

Be Mindful for at least ten minutes each day, using the suggested breathing technique several times a day. We can be mindful doing everyday activities, such as being in the shower, waking up in the morning hearing the birds, and drinking coffee or tea. In what ways have you been increasing your mindfulness?

_____

_____

_____

_____

_____

_____

_____

Meditate every day for ten consecutive days and observe the way it makes you feel. Think of it as an act of self-love and continue meditating daily if you can, even if it is just for 10 minutes. Try out different types of meditations to find the ones that you like, and write down the meditations that you enjoy here.

_____

_____

_____

_____

_____

_____

_____

Write a statement saying how proud you are for taking the steps of active self-care and self-love.

_____

_____

_____

_____

_____

_____

_____

How many people will benefit in your life when you are at your best?

_____

_____

_____

_____

_____

_____

_____

_____

Sunday

Today, I am grateful for . . .

_____

_____

_____

I am proud of myself today because . . .

_____

_____

_____

I practiced self-care ideas today by . . .

_____

_____

_____

I was mindful today by . . .

_____

_____

_____

Today, I used this meditation . . .

_____

_____

_____

Meditating today made me feel . . .

_____

_____

_____

Monday

Today, I am grateful for . . .

_____

_____

_____

I am proud of myself today because . . .

_____

_____

_____

I practiced self-care ideas today by . . .

_____

_____

_____

I was mindful today by . . .

_____

_____

_____

Today, I used this meditation . . .

_____

_____

_____

Meditating today made me feel . . .

_____

_____

_____

Tuesday

Today, I am grateful for . . .

_____

_____

_____

I am proud of myself today because . . .

_____

_____

_____

I practiced self-care ideas today by . . .

_____

_____

_____

I was mindful today by . . .

_____

_____

_____

Today, I used this meditation . . .

_____

_____

_____

Meditating today made me feel . . .

_____

_____

_____

Wednesday

Today, I am grateful for . . .

_____

_____

_____

I am proud of myself today because . . .

_____

_____

_____

I practiced self-care ideas today by . . .

_____

_____

_____

I was mindful today by . . .

_____

_____

_____

Today, I used this meditation . . .

_____

_____

_____

Meditating today made me feel . . .

_____

_____

_____

Thursday

Today, I am grateful for . . .

_____

_____

_____

I am proud of myself today because . . .

_____

_____

_____

I practiced self-care ideas today by . . .

_____

_____

_____

I was mindful today by . . .

_____

_____

_____

Today, I used this meditation . . .

_____

_____

_____

Meditating today made me feel . . .

_____

_____

_____

Friday

Today, I am grateful for . . .

_____

_____

_____

I am proud of myself today because . . .

_____

_____

_____

I practiced self-care ideas today by . . .

_____

_____

_____

I was mindful today by . . .

_____

_____

_____

Today, I used this meditation . . .

_____

_____

_____

Meditating today made me feel . . .

_____

_____

_____

Saturday

Today, I am grateful for . . .

_____

_____

_____

I am proud of myself today because . . .

_____

_____

_____

I practiced self-care ideas today by . . .

_____

_____

_____

I was mindful today by . . .

_____

_____

_____

Today, I used this meditation . . .

_____

_____

_____

Meditating today made me feel . . .

_____

_____

_____

Additional Thoughts

WEEK FIVE REFLECTIONS

I am proud of myself for adding the following tools to my tool belt:

_____

_____

_____

_____

_____

_____

_____

I am being gentle and loving with myself, and I know that every time I am being even a little bit more compassionate with myself it is a success to celebrate. I celebrate the following small successes this week:

_____

_____

_____

_____

_____

_____

_____

Sunday

Today, I am grateful for . . .

_____

_____

_____

I am proud of myself today because . . .

_____

_____

_____

I practiced self-care ideas today by . . .

_____

_____

_____

I was mindful today by . . .

_____

_____

_____

Today, I used this meditation . . .

_____

_____

_____

Meditating today made me feel . . .

_____

_____

_____

Monday

Today, I am grateful for . . .

_____

_____

_____

I am proud of myself today because . . .

_____

_____

_____

I practiced self-care ideas today by . . .

_____

_____

_____

I was mindful today by . . .

_____

_____

_____

Today, I used this meditation . . .

_____

_____

_____

Meditating today made me feel . . .

_____

_____

_____

Tuesday

Today, I am grateful for . . .

_____

_____

_____

I am proud of myself today because . . .

_____

_____

_____

I practiced self-care ideas today by . . .

_____

_____

_____

I was mindful today by . . .

_____

_____

_____

Today, I used this meditation . . .

_____

_____

_____

Meditating today made me feel . . .

_____

_____

_____

Wednesday

Today, I am grateful for . . .

_____

_____

_____

I am proud of myself today because . . .

_____

_____

_____

I practiced self-care ideas today by . . .

_____

_____

_____

I was mindful today by . . .

_____

_____

_____

Today, I used this meditation . . .

_____

_____

_____

Meditating today made me feel . . .

_____

_____

_____

Thursday

Today, I am grateful for . . .

_____

_____

_____

I am proud of myself today because . . .

_____

_____

_____

I practiced self-care ideas today by . . .

_____

_____

_____

I was mindful today by . . .

_____

_____

_____

Today, I used this meditation . . .

_____

_____

_____

Meditating today made me feel . . .

_____

_____

_____

Friday

Today, I am grateful for . . .

_____

_____

_____

I am proud of myself today because . . .

_____

_____

_____

I practiced self-care ideas today by . . .

_____

_____

_____

I was mindful today by . . .

_____

_____

_____

Today, I used this meditation . . .

_____

_____

_____

Meditating today made me feel . . .

_____

_____

_____

Saturday

Today, I am grateful for . . .

_____

_____

_____

I am proud of myself today because . . .

_____

_____

_____

I practiced self-care ideas today by . . .

_____

_____

_____

I was mindful today by . . .

_____

_____

_____

Today, I used this meditation . . .

_____

_____

_____

Meditating today made me feel . . .

_____

_____

_____

Additional Thoughts

WEEK SIX REFLECTIONS

Write down all the ways you are going to care for yourself now to stay balanced and well.

_____

_____

_____

_____

_____

_____

_____

In what ways could you prioritize yourself and your needs this week?

_____

_____

_____

_____

_____

_____

_____

In what ways were you able to take breaks when needed and plan some unstructured restorative time this week?

_____

_____

_____

_____

_____

_____

_____

_____

What types of self-care do you plan on implementing regularly?

_____

_____

_____

_____

_____

_____

_____

_____

When you feel the benefits from implementing the self-care, write down the ways it felt good to meet some of your needs.

_____

_____

_____

_____

_____

_____

_____

_____

Sunday

Today, I am grateful for . . .

_____

_____

_____

I am proud of myself today because . . .

_____

_____

_____

I practiced self-care ideas today by . . .

_____

_____

_____

I was mindful today by . . .

_____

_____

_____

Today, I used this meditation . . .

_____

_____

_____

Meditating today made me feel . . .

_____

_____

_____

Monday

Today, I am grateful for . . .

_____

_____

_____

I am proud of myself today because . . .

_____

_____

_____

I practiced self-care ideas today by . . .

_____

_____

_____

I was mindful today by . . .

_____

_____

_____

Today, I used this meditation . . .

_____

_____

_____

Meditating today made me feel . . .

_____

_____

_____

Tuesday

Today, I am grateful for . . .

_____

_____

_____

I am proud of myself today because . . .

_____

_____

_____

I practiced self-care ideas today by . . .

_____

_____

_____

I was mindful today by . . .

_____

_____

_____

Today, I used this meditation . . .

_____

_____

_____

Meditating today made me feel . . .

_____

_____

_____

Wednesday

Today, I am grateful for . . .

_____

_____

_____

I am proud of myself today because . . .

_____

_____

_____

I practiced self-care ideas today by . . .

_____

_____

_____

I was mindful today by . . .

_____

_____

_____

Today, I used this meditation . . .

_____

_____

_____

Meditating today made me feel . . .

_____

_____

_____

Thursday

Today, I am grateful for . . .

_____

_____

_____

I am proud of myself today because . . .

_____

_____

_____

I practiced self-care ideas today by . . .

_____

_____

_____

I was mindful today by . . .

_____

_____

_____

Today, I used this meditation . . .

_____

_____

_____

Meditating today made me feel . . .

_____

_____

_____

Friday

Today, I am grateful for . . .

_____

_____

_____

I am proud of myself today because . . .

_____

_____

_____

I practiced self-care ideas today by . . .

_____

_____

_____

I was mindful today by . . .

_____

_____

_____

Today, I used this meditation . . .

_____

_____

_____

Meditating today made me feel . . .

_____

_____

_____

Saturday

Today, I am grateful for . . .

_____

_____

_____

I am proud of myself today because . . .

_____

_____

_____

I practiced self-care ideas today by . . .

_____

_____

_____

I was mindful today by . . .

_____

_____

_____

Today, I used this meditation . . .

_____

_____

_____

Meditating today made me feel . . .

_____

_____

_____

Additional Thoughts

WEEK SEVEN REFLECTIONS

Write down all of the positives about your trait.

_____

_____

_____

_____

_____

_____

_____

_____

Name the ways you are proud of these positive qualities.

_____

_____

_____

_____

_____

_____

_____

Sunday

Today, I am grateful for . . .

_____

_____

_____

I am proud of myself today because . . .

_____

_____

_____

I practiced self-care ideas today by . . .

_____

_____

_____

I was mindful today by . . .

_____

_____

_____

Today, I used this meditation . . .

_____

_____

_____

Meditating today made me feel . . .

_____

_____

_____

Monday

Today, I am grateful for . . .

_____

_____

_____

I am proud of myself today because . . .

_____

_____

_____

I practiced self-care ideas today by . . .

_____

_____

_____

I was mindful today by . . .

_____

_____

_____

Today, I used this meditation . . .

_____

_____

_____

Meditating today made me feel . . .

_____

_____

_____

Tuesday

Today, I am grateful for . . .

_____

_____

_____

I am proud of myself today because . . .

_____

_____

_____

I practiced self-care ideas today by . . .

_____

_____

_____

I was mindful today by . . .

_____

_____

_____

Today, I used this meditation . . .

_____

_____

_____

Meditating today made me feel . . .

_____

_____

_____

Wednesday

Today, I am grateful for . . .

_____

_____

_____

I am proud of myself today because . . .

_____

_____

_____

I practiced self-care ideas today by . . .

_____

_____

_____

I was mindful today by . . .

_____

_____

_____

Today, I used this meditation . . .

_____

_____

_____

Meditating today made me feel . . .

_____

_____

_____

Thursday

Today, I am grateful for . . .

_____

_____

_____

I am proud of myself today because . . .

_____

_____

_____

I practiced self-care ideas today by . . .

_____

_____

_____

I was mindful today by . . .

_____

_____

_____

Today, I used this meditation . . .

_____

_____

_____

Meditating today made me feel . . .

_____

_____

_____

Friday

Today, I am grateful for . . .

_____

_____

_____

I am proud of myself today because . . .

_____

_____

_____

I practiced self-care ideas today by . . .

_____

_____

_____

I was mindful today by . . .

_____

_____

_____

Today, I used this meditation . . .

_____

_____

_____

Meditating today made me feel . . .

_____

_____

_____

Saturday

Today, I am grateful for . . .

_____

_____

I am proud of myself today because . . .

_____

_____

I practiced self-care ideas today by . . .

_____

_____

I was mindful today by . . .

_____

_____

Today, I used this meditation . . .

_____

_____

Meditating today made me feel . . .

_____

_____

Additional Thoughts

WEEK EIGHT REFLECTIONS

Read through your journal and write and reflect on all the positives you have uncovered about yourself and your experience as an HSP.

_____

_____

_____

_____

_____

_____

_____

_____

What have you observed that has helped you the most?

_____

_____

_____

_____

_____

_____

_____

What changes will you commit to continuing to do to stay centered and grounded?

_____

_____

_____

_____

_____

_____

_____

_____

What activities are most valuable to you to stay your most balanced self?

_____

_____

_____

_____

_____

_____

_____

_____

Write down the loving-kindness mantras you say to yourself every day. Feel free to create your own too!

_____

_____

_____

_____

_____

_____

_____

What other forms of self-care and self-compassion have you been incorporating into your life?

_____

_____

_____

_____

_____

_____

_____

What areas have you been proud of in helping to reduce your stress numbers?

_____

_____

_____

_____

_____

_____

_____

What activities have you discovered you love to do?

_____

_____

_____

_____

_____

_____

_____

_____

What allows you to fill up your positive tank?

_____

_____

_____

_____

_____

_____

_____

What types of positives have you been focusing on to counteract the brain's negativity bias?

_____

_____

_____

_____

_____

_____

_____

What have you found to be helpful in reducing the sensory overload?

_____

_____

_____

_____

_____

_____

_____

What will you commit to continuing to do to reduce your sensory overload?

_____

_____

_____

_____

_____

_____

_____

_____

Write and reflect on all the positive parts of your trait that you have begun to experience.

_____

_____

_____

_____

_____

_____

_____

What new parts of your trait are you able to enjoy now that you have had this training?

_____

_____

_____

_____

_____

_____

_____

Sunday

Today, I am grateful for . . .

_____

_____

_____

I am proud of myself today because . . .

_____

_____

_____

I practiced self-care ideas today by . . .

_____

_____

_____

I was mindful today by . . .

_____

_____

_____

Today, I used this meditation . . .

_____

_____

_____

Meditating today made me feel . . .

_____

_____

_____

Monday

Today, I am grateful for . . .

_____

_____

_____

I am proud of myself today because . . .

_____

_____

_____

I practiced self-care ideas today by . . .

_____

_____

_____

I was mindful today by . . .

_____

_____

_____

Today, I used this meditation . . .

_____

_____

_____

Meditating today made me feel . . .

_____

_____

_____

Tuesday

Today, I am grateful for . . .

_____

_____

_____

I am proud of myself today because . . .

_____

_____

_____

I practiced self-care ideas today by . . .

_____

_____

_____

I was mindful today by . . .

_____

_____

_____

Today, I used this meditation . . .

_____

_____

_____

Meditating today made me feel . . .

_____

_____

_____

Wednesday

Today, I am grateful for . . .

_____

_____

_____

I am proud of myself today because . . .

_____

_____

_____

I practiced self-care ideas today by . . .

_____

_____

_____

I was mindful today by . . .

_____

_____

_____

Today, I used this meditation . . .

_____

_____

_____

Meditating today made me feel . . .

_____

_____

_____

Thursday

Today, I am grateful for . . .

_____

_____

_____

I am proud of myself today because . . .

_____

_____

_____

I practiced self-care ideas today by . . .

_____

_____

_____

I was mindful today by . . .

_____

_____

_____

Today, I used this meditation . . .

_____

_____

_____

Meditating today made me feel . . .

_____

_____

_____

Friday

Today, I am grateful for . . .

_____

_____

_____

I am proud of myself today because . . .

_____

_____

_____

I practiced self-care ideas today by . . .

_____

_____

_____

I was mindful today by . . .

_____

_____

_____

Today, I used this meditation . . .

_____

_____

_____

Meditating today made me feel . . .

_____

_____

_____

Saturday

Today, I am grateful for . . .

_____

_____

_____

I am proud of myself today because . . .

_____

_____

_____

I practiced self-care ideas today by . . .

_____

_____

_____

I was mindful today by . . .

_____

_____

_____

Today, I used this meditation . . .

_____

_____

_____

Meditating today made me feel . . .

_____

_____

_____

Additional Thoughts

Congratulations!

You have now completed the journals for the HSP brain-training program. Take some time, celebrate, and be proud of the work you have put into this. If you still have areas you want to work on contact me through my website: www.juliebjelland.com. Our journey is never "done," and we are all continually working on ourselves, but I hope you have found that having this companion book has helped you become a more "trained" HSP and that you have met some of your goals and are noticing that you are starting to live better as an HSP. Since we need to continually grow and train ourselves as HSPs, I encourage you to return to your journals to remember and reflect on how you've grown, and you can continue using the additional pages to record your thoughts.

Take really good care of your beautiful HSP self.

All the best,

Julie

Sunday

Today, I am grateful for . . .

_____

_____

_____

_____

_____

_____

I am proud of myself today because . . .

_____

_____

_____

_____

_____

I practiced self-care ideas today by . . .

_____

_____

_____

_____

_____

Monday

Today, I am grateful for . . .

_____

_____

_____

_____

_____

_____

_____

I am proud of myself today because . . .

_____

_____

_____

_____

_____

I practiced self-care ideas today by . . .

_____

_____

_____

_____

_____

Tuesday

Today, I am grateful for . . .

_____

_____

_____

_____

_____

_____

_____

I am proud of myself today because . . .

_____

_____

_____

_____

_____

_____

I practiced self-care ideas today by . . .

_____

_____

_____

_____

_____

Wednesday

Today, I am grateful for . . .

_____

_____

_____

_____

_____

_____

I am proud of myself today because . . .

_____

_____

_____

_____

_____

I practiced self-care ideas today by . . .

_____

_____

_____

_____

_____

Thursday

Today, I am grateful for . . .

_____

_____

_____

_____

_____

_____

I am proud of myself today because . . .

_____

_____

_____

_____

_____

I practiced self-care ideas today by . . .

_____

_____

_____

_____

_____

Friday

Today, I am grateful for . . .

_____

_____

_____

_____

_____

_____

_____

I am proud of myself today because . . .

_____

_____

_____

_____

_____

I practiced self-care ideas today by . . .

_____

_____

_____

_____

_____

Saturday

Today, I am grateful for . . .

_____

_____

_____

_____

_____

_____

_____

I am proud of myself today because . . .

_____

_____

_____

_____

_____

_____

I practiced self-care ideas today by . . .

_____

_____

_____

_____

_____

_____

Sunday

Today, I am grateful for . . .

_____

_____

_____

_____

_____

_____

I am proud of myself today because . . .

_____

_____

_____

_____

_____

I practiced self-care ideas today by . . .

_____

_____

_____

_____

_____

Monday

Today, I am grateful for . . .

_____

_____

_____

_____

_____

_____

_____

I am proud of myself today because . . .

_____

_____

_____

_____

_____

_____

I practiced self-care ideas today by . . .

_____

_____

_____

_____

_____

_____

Tuesday

Today, I am grateful for . . .

_____

_____

_____

_____

_____

_____

I am proud of myself today because . . .

_____

_____

_____

_____

_____

I practiced self-care ideas today by . . .

_____

_____

_____

_____

_____

Wednesday

Today, I am grateful for . . .

_____

_____

_____

_____

_____

_____

I am proud of myself today because . . .

_____

_____

_____

_____

_____

I practiced self-care ideas today by . . .

_____

_____

_____

_____

_____

Thursday

Today, I am grateful for . . .

_____

_____

_____

_____

_____

_____

_____

I am proud of myself today because . . .

_____

_____

_____

_____

_____

I practiced self-care ideas today by . . .

_____

_____

_____

_____

_____

_____

Friday

Today, I am grateful for . . .

_____

_____

_____

_____

_____

_____

_____

I am proud of myself today because . . .

_____

_____

_____

_____

_____

_____

I practiced self-care ideas today by . . .

_____

_____

_____

_____

_____

_____

Saturday

Today, I am grateful for . . .

_____

_____

_____

_____

_____

_____

I am proud of myself today because . . .

_____

_____

_____

_____

_____

I practiced self-care ideas today by . . .

_____

_____

_____

_____

_____

Sunday

Today, I am grateful for . . .

_____

_____

_____

_____

_____

_____

I am proud of myself today because . . .

_____

_____

_____

_____

_____

I practiced self-care ideas today by . . .

_____

_____

_____

_____

_____

Monday

Today, I am grateful for . . .

_____

_____

_____

_____

_____

_____

_____

I am proud of myself today because . . .

_____

_____

_____

_____

_____

_____

I practiced self-care ideas today by . . .

_____

_____

_____

_____

_____

_____

Tuesday

Today, I am grateful for . . .

_____

_____

_____

_____

_____

_____

I am proud of myself today because . . .

_____

_____

_____

_____

_____

I practiced self-care ideas today by . . .

_____

_____

_____

_____

_____

Wednesday

Today, I am grateful for . . .

_____

_____

_____

_____

_____

_____

I am proud of myself today because . . .

_____

_____

_____

_____

_____

I practiced self-care ideas today by . . .

_____

_____

_____

_____

_____

Thursday

Today, I am grateful for . . .

_____

_____

_____

_____

_____

_____

_____

I am proud of myself today because . . .

_____

_____

_____

_____

_____

_____

I practiced self-care ideas today by . . .

_____

_____

_____

_____

_____

_____

Friday

Today, I am grateful for . . .

_____

_____

_____

_____

_____

_____

_____

I am proud of myself today because . . .

_____

_____

_____

_____

_____

_____

I practiced self-care ideas today by . . .

_____

_____

_____

_____

_____

Saturday

Today, I am grateful for . . .

_____

_____

_____

_____

_____

_____

_____

I am proud of myself today because . . .

_____

_____

_____

_____

_____

_____

I practiced self-care ideas today by . . .

_____

_____

_____

_____

_____

_____

Sunday

Today, I am grateful for . . .

_____

_____

_____

_____

_____

_____

I am proud of myself today because . . .

_____

_____

_____

_____

_____

I practiced self-care ideas today by . . .

_____

_____

_____

_____

_____

Monday

Today, I am grateful for . . .

_____

_____

_____

_____

_____

_____

I am proud of myself today because . . .

_____

_____

_____

_____

_____

I practiced self-care ideas today by . . .

_____

_____

_____

_____

_____

Tuesday

Today, I am grateful for . . .

_____

_____

_____

_____

_____

_____

I am proud of myself today because . . .

_____

_____

_____

_____

_____

I practiced self-care ideas today by . . .

_____

_____

_____

_____

_____

Wednesday

Today, I am grateful for . . .

_____

_____

_____

_____

_____

_____

_____

I am proud of myself today because . . .

_____

_____

_____

_____

_____

_____

I practiced self-care ideas today by . . .

_____

_____

_____

_____

_____

_____

Thursday

Today, I am grateful for . . .

_____

_____

_____

_____

_____

_____

I am proud of myself today because . . .

_____

_____

_____

_____

_____

I practiced self-care ideas today by . . .

_____

_____

_____

_____

_____

Friday

Today, I am grateful for . . .

_____

_____

_____

_____

_____

_____

_____

I am proud of myself today because . . .

_____

_____

_____

_____

_____

_____

I practiced self-care ideas today by . . .

_____

_____

_____

_____

_____

_____

Saturday

Today, I am grateful for . . .

_____

_____

_____

_____

_____

_____

_____

I am proud of myself today because . . .

_____

_____

_____

_____

_____

I practiced self-care ideas today by . . .

_____

_____

_____

_____

_____

Additional Thoughts

.

ABOUT THE AUTHOR

Julie is a licensed psychotherapist in California. Having built a successful private practice, Julie continues to expand her reach by developing online brain-training courses, serving as a consultant to other therapists, teaching workshops, and coaching HSPs globally. Her passion and expertise is in neuroscience and determining how to successfully train the brain so people can live their best lives. Her most recent book, *Brain Training for the Highly Sensitive Person: Techniques to Reduce Anxiety and Overwhelming Emotions*, has received outstanding reviews from world-renowned psychologists Tara Brach, PhD, Rick Hanson, PhD, and Ted Zeff, PhD. Julie specializes in working with anxiety and the highly sensitive person (HSP), couple's communication, self-esteem, and the LGBTQQ community. In addition to her work in psychology, she is a former Guide Dogs for the Blind trainer and author of the book *Imagine Life With A Well-Behaved Dog*.

Julie offers many resources for HSPs through her website: www.juliebjelland.com/.

Stay connected to Julie's HSP work and research through her HSP Facebook group: www.facebook.com/HSP.The.Highly.Sensitive.Person/

Made in the USA
Middletown, DE
13 September 2023